ISBN 978-1-330-26852-0
PIBN 10007557

Bernard
Robert
Maxpier
7/6/19

1 MONTH OF
FREE
READING

at

www.ForgottenBooks.com

By purchasing this book you are eligible for one month membership to ForgottenBooks.com, giving you unlimited access to our entire collection of over 1,000,000 titles via our web site and mobile apps.

To claim your free month visit:

www.forgottenbooks.com/free7557

been captured and taken away, they knew not whither. We discovered that this horde of banditti—for in reality and without disguise they were nothing else—was under the leadership of several chiefs, but principally under Karema and Kibunga. They had started sixteen months previously from Wane-Ki-rundu, about thirty miles below Vinya Njara. For eleven months the band had been raiding successfully between the Congo and the Lubiranzi, on the left bank. They had then undertaken to perform the same cruel work between the Biyerre and Wane-Kirundu. On looking at my map, I find that such a territory within the area described would cover superficially 16,200 square geographical miles on the left bank, and 10,500 miles on the right, all of which in statute mileage would he equal to 34,700 square miles, just 2,000 square miles greater than the island of Ireland, inhabited by about one million people. The band when it set out from Kirundu numbered 300 fighting men, armed with flint-locks, double barreled percussion-guns, and a few breech-loaders; their followers or domestic slaves and women doubled this force. Within the en-closure was a series of low sheds extending many lines deep from the immediate edge of the clay bank inland, 100 yards; in length; the camp was about three hundred yards; at the landing place below were fifty-four long canoes, varying in carrying capacity. Each might convey from ten to one hundred people. The first general impressions are that the camp is much too densely peopled for comfort. There are rows upon rows of dark nakedness, relieved here and there by the white dresses of the captors. There are lines or groups of naked forms—upright, standing, or moving about listlessly; naked bodies are stretched under the sheds in all positions; naked legs innumerable are seen in the perspec-tive of prostrate sleepers; there are countless naked children—many mere infants—forms of boyhood and girlhood, and occasionally a drove of absolutely naked old women bending under a basket of fuel, or cassava-tubers, or bana-nas, who are driven through the moving groups by two or three musketeers. On paying more attention to details, I observed that mostly all are fettered; youths with iron rings around their necks, through which a chain, like one of our boat anchor-chains, is rove, securing the captives by twenties. The children over ten are secured by these copper rings, each ringed leg brought together by the central ring, which accounts for the apparent listlessness of movement I observed on first coming in presence of this curious scene. The mothers are se-cured by shorter chains, around whom their respective progeny of infants are grouped, hiding the cruel iron links that fall in loops or festoons on their mam-mas' breasts. There is not an adult man captive among them. The slave trad-ers admit they have only 2,300 captives in this fold, yet they have raided through the length and breadth of a country larger than Ireland, bringing fire and spreading carnage with lead and iron. Both banks of the river show that 118 villages and 43 districts have been devastated, out of which is only educed this scanty profit of 2,300 females and children, and about 2,000 tusks of ivory; the spears, swords, bows, and the quivers of arrows show that many adults have fallen. Given that 118 villages were peopled only by 1,000 each, we have only a profit of two per cent, and by the time all these captives have

SLAVERY IN AFRICA.

By HENRY DRUMMOND.

[Reprinted, by permission, from the pages of SCRIBNERS MAGAZINE, June, 1889.]

THE closing years of the nineteenth century will present to the future a moral phenomenon unique in history, the rise of a great, unselfish International Movement for the abolition of a single wrong—a wrong which endangers no international interest, which affects personally none of those engaged in crushing it, which is dealt with purely on the ground of humanity and Christianity. The greater Governments of Europe are just now combined in forming, not the usual defensive alliance to enrich themselves or diminish the risks of war to those they love and guard, but an offensive alliance to save the land of a stranger who has no claim but his utter helplessness. And what is of greater significance still, the Roman Catholic and the Protestant Churches have met for once on a common ground, and find themselves fighting side by side for the redemption of a country beyond the pale of either. When before did the nations of the world direct their politics, without the desire of acquisition, to a people which was not even a nation, or the ecclesiastics devote themselves, without the hope of a proselyte, to a land without a church?

A spectacle of this importance deserves more than a passing notice, and I shall try in the following pages to present a bird's-eye view of the movement, the nature of the evil against which it is directed, and the steps that are being taken for its remedy.

Notwithstanding the recent influx of explorers, Africa is still almost an unexplored land. Its condition is really known only by what a geologist would "sections"—lines of survey, struck at several widely different points, with ss-sections here and there connecting them; and it is only by inference from the great travel-routes that the moral and civil structure of the country can be out. But, from the fatal unanimity upon one or two cardinal points among various observers, and from the constant corroboration of their facts by sh explorers, there is but too much reason to fear that these sections are typical of the whole, and that the darkness of the Dark Continent must be held to be unrelieved at no single spot. A very brief citation, therefore, of one or two of the more important witnesses will place the facts before the imagination in all their lurid truth and nakedness.

A few years ago the well-known German explorer, Captain Wissmann, found himself within a few degrees of the equator, in the heart of Africa. It was a region of great beauty and fertility, with forests and rivers, and great and many-peopled towns. The inhabitants were quiet and peaceable, and lived a life of artless simplicity and happiness. For generations they had been established there; they grew many fruits in their gardens, and excelled in the manufacture of cloth, pottery, ironware, and wood-carving. No Arab slaver had ever visited this country. Within its borders the very report of a gun had never once been heard. But as the explorer walked among the palm-trees and met the kindly eyes of the country-people who came to gaze upon the white man, his heart sank. This Arcadia could not last. He knew, from what had happened in adjacent districts, from what happens every day in Africa, that its fate was sealed.

And the sequel showed too clearly that his silent prophecy was right. Four years passed. The same traveler led his caravan once more across this sylvan country. "As we approached the villages we wondered that no one came out to receive us with rejoicings, that no merry laughter greeted our ears. We entered the deep shade of the mighty palms, and to the right and left were the clearings where our friends had stood. Tall grass had overgrown all that formerly gladdened us. The crops were destroyed; everything was laid waste. The silence of death breathes over the lofty crowns of the palms waving in the wind. We enter, and it is in vain we look for the happy homesteads and happy old scenes. A charred pole here and there, a few banana-trees, are the only evidences that man once dwelt here. Bleached skulls by the road-side, and the skeletons of human hands attached to poles, tell the story of what has happened since our last visit." Some wretched fugitives from them supplied the missing links in the story. "People with long white shirts and wearing cloth round their heads (the Arabs) had been there with their chief, who was called Tippu Tib. He at first came to trade, then he had stolen and carried away the women. Those who had opposed him had been cut down or shot, and the greater part of the natives had fled to the ravines and forests. The Arabs had remained in the place in force, as long as there was any chance of hunting and finally capturing the fugitives in the woods. What they could not utilize they had destroyed or set fire to—in a word, everything had been laid waste. Then they passed on. The fugitives had returned to their former homes, and had endeavored to cultivate and renew their fields, and rebuild what was possible. After three months Tippu Tib's hordes had again appeared, and the same scenes had been re-enacted, and again, for a third time, three months later. Famine and the greatest misery had been thereby produced throughout all the country of the Beneki. In Africa the results of famine are found mostly in the shape of frightful epidemics, especially smallpox. I was told that a few of the fugitives had escaped to the West, but only an imperceptibly small number in comparison with those thousands—I may almost say millions—that I had found there on my first visit."

These statements, told by Wissmann himself to a meeting at Cologne, in October, 1888, might be paralleled by almost any traveler who has any experience of remoter Africa. The following account, by Mr. Fred M. Moir, of the African Lakes Company, refers to a totally different district, and I select it, not so much to emphasize the horrors of slavery, but to illustrate the Arab slaver's general policy and his method of setting to work.

"Within twenty miles of the station, while we were on our march from Nyassa to Tanganyika, the fertile valley of the Lofu was the scene of a terrible slave raid. An Arab, Kabunda, who had been settled there for about ten years, having many houses and slaves, determined to go to Zanzibar with his ivory. So he picked a quarrel with Katimbwe, the chief, and took all his cattle ; then organized a sudden raid throughout all the valley, and every man, woman and child who could be found was seized and tied up. Very few managed to escape him or his keen hunters, and a caravan was made up for the coast ; but the smiling valley that had been known as the Garden of the Tanganyika, from its fertility and the industry of its people, now silent and desolate, was added to that already long stretch of hungry wilderness through which we had passed."

But this is only the first act of the drama. With the slave march to the coast the real tragedy begins. Here is the procession which a few days afterward filed past Mr. Moir's tent :

"First came armed men, dancing, gesticulating and throwing about their guns, as only Arabs can do, to the sound of drums, panpipes, and other less musical instruments. Then followed, slowly and sedately, the great man himself, accompanied by his brother and other head men, his richly caparisoned donkey walking along near by ; and surely no greater contrast can be conceived than that between this courteous, white-robed Arab, with his gold embroidered joho, silver sword and daggers, and silken turban, and the miserable swarm of naked, squalid, human beings that he had wantonly dragged from their now ruined homes in order to enrich himself. Behind the Arab came groups of wives and household servants, laughing and talking as they passed along, carrying the camp utensils and other impedimenta of their masters. After that the main rabble of the caravan, the men armed with guns, spears and axes. Ominously prominent among the loads were many slave-sticks, to be handy if any turned refractory or if any likely stranger were met. Mingling with, and guarded by them, came the wretched, overburdened, tied-up slaves. The men who might still have had spirit to try and escape were driven, tied two-and-two, in the terrible goree or taming stick, or in gangs of about a dozen, each with an iron collar let into a long iron chain, many, even so soon after the start, staggering under their loads. And the women ! I can hardly trust myself to think or speak of them—they were fastened to chains or thick bark ropes ; very many, in addition to their heavy weight of grain or ivory, carried little brown babies, dear to their hearts as a white man's child to his. The double burden was almost too much, and still they struggled wearily on, knowing too well that when they showed signs of fatigue, not the slaver's ivory, but the living child would be torn from them and thrown aside to die. One poor old woman I could not help noticing. She was carrying a biggish boy who should have been walking, but whose thin, weak legs had evidently given way ; she was tottering already; it was the supreme effort of a mother's love—and all in vain ; for the child, easily recognizable, was brought into camp a couple of hours later by one of my hunters, who had found him on the path. We had him cared for, but his poor mother would never know. Already, during the three days' journey from Liendwe, death had been freeing the captives. It was well for them ; still we could not help shuddering as, in the darkness, we heard the howl of the hyenas along the track."

According to the usual computation of travelers, the mortality during the slave march from the interior to the coast is set down at fifty per cent. In some cases it may be less, but in others it is undoubtedly more, the difference depending on climate, the nature of the country traversed, and especially the use to which the slaves are to be put when they reach their destination. In some caravans the able-bodied men receive all the attention, the other slaves being left to struggle on and live or die as it may be. In others, the women and children alone are needed, while the men, as a possible source of danger, are either killed or allowed to escape. In either case the loss of life by cruelty, starvation, fatigue, or murder, is an element in framing a count against the slave trade which must be seriously considered.

No one who understands how human life is estimated by savage peoples will doubt the shocking and revolting accounts of travelers regarding this phase of the traffic ; and no one who knows what an Arab's heart is made of will make any discount even for the exaggeration of an orator, as he listens to the following citation from a speech delivered the other day in London by Cardinal Lavigerie.

"The men who appear the strongest, and whose escape is to be feared, have their hands tied, and sometimes their feet, in such fashion that walking becomes a torture to them ; and on their necks are placed yokes which attach several of them together. They march all day ; at night, when they stop to rest, a few handfuls of raw 'sorgho' are distributed among the captives. This is all their food. Next morning they must start again. But after the first day or two the fatigue, the sufferings, and the privations have weakened a great many. The women and the aged are the first to halt. Then, in order to strike terror into this miserable mass of human beings, their conductors, armed with a wooden bar to economize powder, approach those who appear to be the most exhausted and deal them a terrible blow on the nape of the neck. The unfortunate victims utter a cry, and fall to the ground in the convulsions of death. The terrified troop immediately resumes its march. Terror has imbued even the weakest with new strength. Each time some one breaks down, the same horrible scene is repeated. At night, on arriving at their halting-place, after the first days of such a life, a not less frightful scene awaits them. The traffickers in human flesh have acquired by experience a knowledge of how much their victims can endure. A glance shows them those who will soon sink from weariness ; then, to economize the scanty food which they distribute, they pass behind these wretched beings and fell them with a single blow. Their corpses remain where they fall, when they are not suspended on the branches of the neighboring trees ; and it is close to them that their companions are obliged to eat and to sleep. But what sleep ! it may be easily imagined. Among the young negroes snatched by us from this hell and restored to liberty, there are some who, long afterward, wake up every night, shrieking fearfully. They behold again, in their dreams, the abominable and bloody scenes which they have witnessed. In this manner the weary tramp continues—sometimes for months, when the caravan comes from a distance. Their number diminishes daily. If, goaded by their cruel sufferings, some attempt to rebel or to escape, their fierce masters cut them down with their swords, and leave them as they lie along the road, attached to one another by their yokes. Therefore it has been truly said that, if a traveler lost the way leading from Equatorial Africa to the towns where slaves are sold, he could easily find it again by the skeletons of the negroes with which it is strewed."

Cardinal Lavigerie, be it remembered, does not speak here as the mere rhetorician. As Archbishop of Algiers, he knows Africa personally. As Roman Catholic Primate of Africa, he is in ceaseless communication with the missionaries of his Church in the Sahara region, the Upper Congo, and the Great Lakes from the south of Tanganyika to the sources of the Nile. "Our missionaries at Tanganyika write to us," he says, "that there is not a single day in which they do not see pass caravans of slaves which have been brought from afar as carriers for the ivory, or from the markets of the interior, like human cattle. Never in any part of the known world, or in the pages of its history, has there been such butchery and murder, and such contempt for human life. Already millions of human beings have thus been murdered during the last quarter of a century, but the numbers increase continually, and on the high plateaux of the interior the figures given by our missionaries surpass those given by Cameron for the slave trade of the Zambesi and Nyassa."

One would have thought the figures of Cameron here referred to impossible to beat. "Every minute," he wrote lately in a magazine, "a fresh victim is seized on by the slave stealers; not an hour passes without more than fifty being killed or torn from their homes; and during this month of August, in which I write, forty-five thousand more victims are being added to the number of those who appeal to us for aid and protection from some of the foulest criminals that ever disgraced the earth."

I should willingly spare the reader the suffering of further acquaintance with the actual facts of the slave trade, but I am compelled, before closing the evidence, to recall one long dark passage from Mr. Stanley's book on the Congo. The stress of this question must always lie, not upon its advocates but simply on its witnesses, and the importance of Mr. Stanley's testimony forms its own apology for the extreme length of the following quotation :

"Our guide, Yumbila, was told to question them as to what was the cause of this dismal scene, and an old man stood out and poured forth his tale of grief and woe with an exceeding volubility. He told of a sudden and unexpected invasion of their village, by a host of leaping, yelling men in the darkness, who dinned their ears with murderous fusillades, slaughtering their people as they sprang out of their burning huts into the light of the flames. Not a third of the men had escaped; the larger number of the women and children had been captured and taken away, they knew not whither. We discovered that this horde of banditti—for in reality and without disguise they were nothing else —was under the leadership of several chiefs, but principally under Karema and Kibunga. They had started sixteen months previously from Wane-Kirundu, about thirty miles below Vinya Njara. For eleven months the band had been raiding successfully between the Congo and the Lubiranzi, on the left bank. They had then undertaken to perform the same cruel work between the Biyerre and Wane-Kirundu. On looking at my map, I find that such a territory within the area described would cover superficially 16,200 square geographical miles on the left bank, and 10,500 miles on the right, all of which in statute mileage would be equal to 34,700 square miles, just 2,000 square miles greater than the island of Ireland, inhabited by about one million people. The band when it set out from Kirundu numbered 300 fighting men, armed with flint-locks, double barreled percussion-guns, and a few breech-loaders; their followers or domestic slaves and women doubled this force. Within the enclosure was a series of low sheds extending many lines deep from the immediate edge of the clay bank inland, 100 yards; in length, the camp was about three hundred yards; at the landing place below were fifty-four long canoes, varying in carrying capacity. Each might convey from ten to one hundred people. The first general impressions are that the camp is much too densly peopled for comfort. There are rows upon rows of dark nakedness, relieved here and there by the white dresses of the captors. There are lines or groups of naked forms —upright, standing, or moving about listlessly; naked bodies are stretched under the sheds in all positions; naked legs innumerable are seen in the perspective of prostrate sleepers; there are countless naked children--many mere infants—forms of boyhood and girlhood, and occasionally a drove of absolutely naked old women bending under a basket of fuel, or cassava-tubers, or bananas, who are driven through the moving groups by two or three musketeers. On paying more attention to details, I observed that mostly all are fettered; youths with iron rings around their necks, through which a chain, like one of our boat anchor-chains, is rove, securing the captives by twenties. The children over ten are secured by these copper rings, each ringed leg brought together by the central ring, which accounts for the apparent listlessness of movement I observed on first coming in presence of this curious scene. The mothers are secured by shorter chains, around whom their respective progeny of infants are grouped, hiding the cruel iron links that fall in loops or festoons on their mammas' breasts. There is not an adult man captive among them. The slave traders admit they have only 2,300 captives in this fold, yet they have raided through the length and breadth of a country larger than Ireland, bringing fire and spreading carnage with lead and iron. Both banks of the river show that 118 villages and 43 districts have been devastated, out of which is only educed this scanty profit of 2,300 females and children, and about 2,000 tusks of ivory! the spears, swords, bows, and the quivers of arrows show that many adults have fallen. Given that 118 villages were peopled only by 1,000 each, we have only a profit of two per cent., and by the time all these captives have been subjected to the accidents of the river-voyage to Kirundu and Nyangwe, of camp-life and its harsh miseries, to the havoc of small-pox, and the pests which miseries breed, there will only remain a scant one per cent. upon the bloody venture. They tell me, however, that the convoys already arrived at Nyangwe with slaves captured in the interior have been as great as their present band. Five expeditions have come and gone with their booty of ivory and slaves, and these five expeditions have now completely weeded the large territory described above. If each expedition has been as successful as this, the slave traders have been enabled to obtain 5,000 women and children safe to Nyangwe, Kirundu, and Vibondo, above the Stanley Falls. This 5,000 out of an annual million will be at the rate of a half per cent., or 5 slaves out of 1,000 people. This is poor profit out of such large waste of life, for originally we assume the slaves to have mustered about ten thousand in number. To obtain the 2,300 slaves out of the 118 villages they must have shot a round number of 2,500 people, while 1,300 men died by the way-side through scant provisions and the intensity of their hopeless wretchedness. How many are wounded and die in the forest or droop to death through an overwhelming sense of their calamities we do not know; but if the above figures are trustworthy, then the outcome from the territory with its million of souls is 5,000 slaves, obtained at the cruel expense of 33,000 lives! And such slaves! They are females or young children who cannot run away, or who with youthful indifference will soon forget the terrors of their capture! Yet each of the very smallest infants has cost the life of a father, and perhaps his three stout brothers and three grown-up daughters. An entire family of six souls have been done to death to obtain that small, feeble, useless child. These are my thoughts as I look upon the horrible scene. Every second during which I regard them the clink of fetters and chains strikes upon my ears. My eyes catch sight of that continual lifting of the hand to ease the neck in the collar, or as it displays a manacle exposed through a muscle being irritated by its weight or want of fitness. My nerves are offended with the rancid effluvium of the unwashed herds within this human kennel. The smell of other abominations annoys me in that vitiated atmosphere. For how could poor people, bound and riveted together by twenties, do otherwise than wallow in filth? Only the old women are taken out to forage. They dig out the cassava-tubers and search for the banana; while the guard, with musket ready, keenly watches for the coming of the revengeful native. Not much food can be procured in this manner, and what is obtained is flung down in a heap before each gang to at once cause an unseemly scramble. Many of these poor things have been already months fettered in this manner, and their bones stand out in bold relief in the attenuated skin which hangs down in thin wrinkles and puckers."

It is enough. Our hearts are sick with slaughter. Let the witnesses stand down. Is the smoke of this torment to go up for ever and ever? Remember that these deeds of blood and darkness are no isolated facts, no temporary misfortunes, no mere passing accidents of the savage state. They are samples of a sustained, accepted, and carefully organized system of cruelty and murder which pervades and penetrates every corner of this continent. Do not let it be supposed that this horror is over, that this day of tribulation is at an end. This horror and this day are now. It is not even abating. *Slavery is on the increase.* Time, civilization, Christianity are not really touching it. No fact in relation to the slave trade is more appalling than this. The fact of this increase, for a time denied, then doubted, has at last been reluctantly admitted, even by the Government of England. In a Government Blue-book issued only the other day, Her Majesty's consul for the Somali Coast reports that "the slave trade has been very active of late. On the 16th of September (1888), Captain Gissing captured three dhows and brought two hundred and four slaves to Aden." The consul at Zanzibar writes (September, 1888) to the Marquis of Salisbury: " There is a marked increase in the slave traffic carried on under the protection of the French flag." The consul further states that dhows carrying French colors were constantly and regularly leaving for the Comoro Islands, Mayotta, and Madagascar, loaded with slaves. In June, 1888, Brigadier-General Hogg, dating from the Aden Residency, wrote to the Bombay Government: "I have the honor to bring to the notice of Government that I have from time to time received reports of the activity of the slave trade from the neighborhood of the Gulf of Tajourra, and I deem it my duty to inform Government of this fact with a view to such action being taken as may be deemed advisable." Turning to a very different region, we find Consul O'Neill addressing a letter to the Marquis of Salisbury with reference to the coast of Mozambique: "I have the honor to say that with the opinion that the East African slave trade has received some considerable impulse, and has greatly increased and strengthened, I am compelled regretfully but entirely to concur. The evidence I have myself received from the interior is of a similar nature." The Portuguese authorities in that district concur in these statements. Thus the commandant of the lately established military post of Mji Mkwali, in his monthly report of the state of the province, calmly writes, under the heading "Commerce": "The sole trade of this district, at the present, is in slaves."

The cause of this revived activity of the slave trade is not far to seek. It is the normal expansion of a paying business. More men engage in it; more capital is invested in it. The Arab never retires from business. With the profits of his first small caravan he equips and heads a larger one. As the years pass, his flying columns grow larger and larger, and fiercer and fiercer. Now he can attack with impunity a region which, in former days, he must have let alone. Formerly he fraternized and traded with the great interior nations; now he overthrows and carries them off bodily. Having much capital and better fire-arms he can push farther and farther into the country, establishing depots as he goes, which become minor centres of the trade. Long ago the Arab dared not venture beyond a limited distance from the coast-line. Now he pervades and almost dominates the continent. As one region after another is drained of its slaves and ivory, fresh and remoter fields have to be sought out. So home after home is made desolate, region after region is ravished, state after state is demolished, nation after nation is mowed down like grass. Such being and invite disaster; to be poor is to be the prey of the first murdering Arab who happens to pass that way.

Where do the slaves go to? What is their final market and destination? These questions are among the first to be asked by those whose interest is awakened in the slave trade, and the answers are not so easy to put together. In the first place, multitudes are used up as mere beasts of burden. The mortality in a slave-caravan has already been referred to. Now, in all cases where a slave who is a carrier or porter succumbs on the march, a fresh man has to be secured from some neighboring tribe to carry on his load. Vacancies caused by desertion are supplied in the same way. The vacancies caused among the local tribes due to the filling up of these vacancies, again, have to be supplied by fresh seizures of slaves from surrounding tribes, so that a perpetual circulation of this human currency is set in motion. Again, the domestic slaves of the coast-regions were for a long time drained away by shipment from the various slaving ports. The supply throughout vast littoral territories was thus exhausted, and had to be continuously replenished from caravans arriving from the interior. These domestic slaves were absolutely necessary to the coast-tribes for household and agricultural purposes, and there can be no doubt that enormous numbers of slaves have lately been absorbed to replace those exported from the littoral zone at earlier periods.

But, in addition to this, it is an open secret that several large and defined markets for slaves exist in many parts of Africa and in the adjoining islands. Off the Zanzibar coast, for instance, the extensive plantations of Pemba are wrought by slave-labor. Owing to the nature of the work and the fatal insalubrity of the climate the death-rate here is terrible, and a ceaseless traffic with the coast has to be kept up to supply the almost daily blanks. The slavers of the Mozambique Channel find a ready market in the Comoro Islands, and even in Madagascar. Abyssinia, again, has many slave-markets, the slaves being taken overland to Roheita, on the south of Assab Bay, whence they are shipped during the night in dhows to Jeddah, Hodeida, and elsewhere in Arabia. Turning to the north of the continent, we find that almost every town in Morocco is furnished with its slave market. A few years ago these markets existed in all the Mediterranean provinces, and they are still in active life everywhere south of the European boundaries. In a word, it may be said that almost every Mohammedan town in the country is a receiving and distributing centre for slaves.

What, now, is being done to cope with this far-reaching and still-growing wrong? That a cry so piteous and awful should have long ago wrung the heart of the civilized world was to be expected. Let us see in how many ways and from what diverse sources the needed help begins to come. Many great and powerful agencies are already enlisted in this cause, and some are actually embarked upon the struggle. These fall into four classes—philanthropic, political, military, and commercial; but, from the way in which their various interests are linked together, it will not be possible to separate them in making a few remarks upon each.

In the foremost rank among those to receive honorable mention in contending with the slave trade must be placed that venerable and influential institution, the British and Foreign Anti-slavery Society. This society has made it its one aim to focus public attention upon the evils of slavery in every part of the world, and, by agitation at public meetings, by the steady dissemination of literature, and by the personal influence of its few but devoted members, has formed and guided public and parliamentary opinion in England throughout a long course of years. Its monthly magazine, the *Anti-slavery Reporter*, of which the eighth volume of a fourth series lies before me as I write, is the classic of slavery literature, and contains a storehouse of carefully sifted facts upon every aspect of the question. The creed of the society may be gathered from a single clause of its constitution :

"That, so long as *slavery* exists, there is no reasonable prospect of the annihilation of the *slave trade*, and of extinguishing the sale and barter of human beings ; that the extinction of slavery and the slave trade will be attained most effectually by the employment of those means which are *of a moral, religious, and pacific character;* and that no measures be resorted to by this Society, in the prosecution of these objects, but such as are in entire accordance with these principles."

With the first two clauses of this sentence most men will be, in the main, agreed. The abolition of the *status* of slavery, could that be brought about, would of course annihilate the slave trade. But how could that be brought about? By a Declaration, it is said—a Declaration by all the European powers, including Turkey, in International Conference assembled, that the *status* of slavery was no longer to be recognized, and that therefore any traffic in this commodity must be held as contraband or piratical and punished accordingly. But held contraband by whom? Punished by whom? Enforced by whom? Would not the mere attempt to enforce this throughout the vast territories of the Dark Continent demand the resort to physical force, at least at some point? Not that the thing is not worth trying. In some quarters it would certainly do good. For even some of the European powers are themselves not above suspicion in the matter of countenancing, or at least winking at, the existence of slavery under the shadow of their own flag. But the bulk of the African tribes have no flag, in the political sense. And even where an European power has raised its standard over a native territory, its own existence there is in most cases too precarious to be periled by any serious attempt to extirpate so ancient a custom as that, for instance, of domestic slavery. That the abolition of the *status* of slavery would be a valuable auxiliary to those means of a "moral, religious, and pacific character" which the Society recommends is not to be disputed. That *in time*, also, these means would together bring about the end will be denied by no one who knows how the leaven of Christianity has wrought in history. But meantime? Are we to stand by and let chance after chance escape us of decisive action at particular points? As emergencies rise, are we not to meet them? As favorable opportunities open of closing markets or of snatching the prey from the very arms of the slaver, are we not to utilize the forces and resources of civilization effectual for that purpose? The slaver cannot be caught *in flagrante delicto* and dealt with effectively without the show, and, if necessary, the application of forces other than moral. The Anti-slavery Society would itself countenance punishment before a formal tribunal after the practice of slavery has been declared illegal. But till that hour has come, an informal tribunal must take its place, and the way be paved for the introduction of the more peaceful, more permanent, and more beneficent influences so justly advocated by it.

At this moment a freshly organized slaving centre has just been erected in the heart of one of the most hopeful districts in Africa—the north end of Lake Nyassa. Civilizing and missionary agencies, after years of work, and after the most serious cost in lives and money, were just beginning to tell upon that country. But everything is now disorganized, paralyzed and put to confusion; and till these Arab intruders are driven from their intrenchment no further progress can be dreamed of. The very existence of the tribes who are there being worked upon is threatened, and those who know the local conditions intimately are compelled, against all their previous policy and inclinations, to call for the help of arms. Fortunately this cry for help has been heard by willing ears, and a Nyassa Defence Fund is now being raised in Scotland to deal practically with this special crisis.

But it is evident that if action along this line is to be taken at all it must not be local or temporary or spasmodic, but an organized system with ramifications in every quarter of the continent. And hence schemes of a larger kind are being discussed. The general basis of these proposals is to have armed boats on the great inland lakes, with depots of men here and there who would act as a sort of police-patrol. To be more than child's-play such schemes would have to be international in character; and co-operation between all the countries and agencies at work in Africa would be a first condition of success.

Two things give one hope that some such scheme may yet take definite shape. The first is the formation of Anti-slavery Societies all over Europe. Mainly as the result of the noble crusade of Cardinal Lavigerie, these societies are now organized in Germany, France, and Belgium, and others are following in Italy, Spain, and other countries of Europe. Large sums of money are pouring into their treasuries, Pope Leo XIII. having headed the subscription lists with a donation of 300,000 francs. What the policy of these various societies may be remains to be seen, but the mere awakening of an interest so widespread and practical must be an important factor in the solution of the problem.

The second hopeful sign is the adoption of the anti-slavery policy by the German Reichstag, and its co-operation with England in the blockade of the Zanzibar coast. Germany has a great and momentous future in relation to this question. Vast tracts of Africa are now under her wing, and if she rises to her opportunity immediate progress may be made. But the practical interest of

England and Germany must not be limited to this. Merely to operate on the coast is not even to half do the work. The real mischief is in the interior. It is there the Arab must be dealt with; and even apart from that Arab slavery which finds its main outlet at the various seaports, the raiding of African chief against chief and of larger tribe against weaker is in some regions almost as bad. Nowhere is there any real security to the native either of life or property; and the whole country, in a word, requires administration. Any scheme, therefore, which is permanently to improve the country must strike at once for its heart. And on the whole, and until the various colonizing and missionary agencies have begun to tell upon the lives and habits of the people, the establishment of some definite police administration throughout the interior seems to be the most rational policy.

We say police administration, rather than military. An international military system would be almost impossible in practice, but that is not the main reason. It would be of the first importance to teach both African and Arab the distinction between a police and a military system. The policeman is a protector, the soldier is an avenger—so, at least, it would be in Africa. Soldiers would necessarily be regarded as enemies; with wise and patient management police-patrols might come to be looked upon as guardians of the peace. The worst thing that could possibly happen, either for the slave trade, for the African, or for the European in Africa, would be the letting loose upon this continent of expeditions of mere fighting men who from time to time would raid across the country and leave behind them only a trail of blood and hate. To do this is so easy; its cheap glory seems so real; an immediate end is sometimes served— these things are the temptation of the man who has power in Africa. But no man should be given power in Africa who has not learned the greater power of self-control, of a policy of patience, of the wisdom of quiet work for large and possibly remote ends. A sensational success may here and there bring momentary relief, but only a large, kindly, and restrained effort, carried out by men whose heads are cool and whose hearts are warm, can ever emancipate Africa.

What we look for, then, for Africa is a limited occupation, the most limited conceivable, of picked men, who would ingratiate themselves with the various tribes, who would explain their mission everywhere as they went, and give the Arab to understand that they were there for a single purpose. What the native tribes really want is leaders, and access to the munitions of modern warfare. Both of these would be supplied if necessary from the proposed depots, but the mere presence of these agencies in the country would probably render actual warfare an exceptional circumstance.

But the best result would be that under the moral and physical support of these agents the various civilizing, colonizing, trading, and missionary enterprises would advance with rapid strides and overrun the country—in time replacing the very agents which fostered them into being. It is to these enterprises that we are to look for the lasting good to Africa, the military or police element being only an unfortunate preliminary necessity. The men to whom this adventurous and benevolent commission would be given would be selected persons, lay and military, from the different nations interested in the pacification of Africa. Some of these would be paid, others might be volunteers. Is there any reason why a few young men, whom Fate, kind or unkind, has rendered independent as regards pecuniary and domestic ties, should not espouse this holy cause and find a fitting career for at least a few of the stronger years of their life in delivering this nation of children from their long Reign of Terror? The rank and file of the patrol-corps, under their leadership, might be largely Africans, or even natives of India, judiciously chosen and trained to handle a gun. But the ball only needs to be set rolling. There is knowledge enough in the world of African ways and habits to guarantee the details.

Such ideas as these are already possessing the public mind in England. Everywhere meetings are being held to discuss this question. The Government, the Church, and the most famous names in the country are interested in it; and the time for action on the large scale cannot be far away.

What will America do to help? Time was when the United States kept a cruiser on the west coast of Africa to check this trade. But when the attitude of America to the Congo treaty is remembered, and her refusal to touch the question of the exportation to Africa of arms, ammunition and liquor, can it be said that she keeps her place to-day in that moral reformation of the world which is the duty and privilege of all the foremost nations? Is it true of that Constitution of which she is so worthily proud, that with reference to these questions, and in the words of the Prime Minister of England: "They (the United States) have told us that, owing to the peculiarities of their Constitution, they are not very anxious to enter into obligations with foreign powers"? America has never been provincial. She must not become so. So manifold and pressing are now the interests of her own great country that she might also be pardoned if she did. But the world will be bewildered and disappointed if she separates herself now from the rest of mankind in facing those great wrongs of humanity from which seas cannot divide her and which her poorer brethren in every part of Europe are giving themselves to relieve. America does well in refusing the entanglements of European politics. Let her be careful lest she isolate herself from its humanities. None who know her will fear for a moment that the breadth of her sympathies and the greatness of her national heart will not continue to be shown in her sustained philanthropies, in her joining hand to hand with the advanced nations of the earth in helping on all universal causes which find their appeal in the world's great need and tribulation.